I0777180

The Story of a Special Day
Volume 219

August
6

The 218th day of the year (219th in leap years). There are 147 days remaining until the end of the year.

by Michael Dobson

Timespinner
Press

This book is also available in e-book form for Kindle, e-pub devices, and other formats from your favorite online booksellers.

For more information about the series, about us, or about your special day, please email us at editor@timespinnerpress.com.

Look for other volumes in *The Story of a Special Day,* coming often. See www.timespinnerpress.com for details and for the most recent information.

Table of Contents

For the definition of "O.S.," "N.S.," "CE," and "BCE" used with some dates , see the section "On Names and Dates."

Cover: A "selfie" taken by NASA's Mars rover *Curiosity,* which landed on the Red Planet August 6, 2012 — the **Cover Story.**

Quote of the Day

"Never neglect an extraordinary appearance or happening. It may be — usually is, in fact — a false alarm that leads to nothing, but may on the other hand be the clue provided by fate to lead you to some important advance."

Alexander Fleming, discoverer of penicillin, born August 6, 1881

Today
in
History
August 6

The Moon of Sturgeon August, P. D. Beckwith

What Happened on August 6?

While some days of the year are more famous than others, every day of the year is filled with important, exciting, and unusual events, from religious awakenings to natural disasters, from wars to breakthroughs in technology, and from tragedy to triumph.

In this section, you'll learn about all the events that make August 6 important, including the special event that makes up our cover story or event of the day. Some events you may already know about, others may be new to you, but all of them are important parts of the history of the work.

Let's explore some of the reasons why August 6 is a very special day!

The mushroom cloud over Hiroshima, The column is about 20,000 feet high while the ground smoke covers some 10,000 feet. (Photo: SSGT George R. Caron, tail gunner aboard *Enola Gay*.)

Event of the Day
Atomic Bombing of Hiroshima (1945)

On August 6, 1945, the first use of nuclear weapons in war took place, when the United Staes dropped a uranium bomb (nicknamed "Little Boy") on the city of Hiroshima, Japan. The death toll is uncertain; estimates range from 90,000 to 146,000 people. About half died immediately; the others suffered varying degrees of radiation sickness and died between weeks and months later.

With the surrender of Nazi Germany on May 8, Japan was the only remaining active Axis power. For some time, US planners had been organizing an invasion of Japan, code named Operation Downfall.[*] The Japanese planned an all-out defense, and casualties on both sides were expected to be massive.

The US carried out an extensive bombing campaign to weaken anticipated resistance. The firebombing of Tokyo, code named Operation Meetinghouse, killed an estimated 100,000 Japanese in a single night, the single deadliest bombing raid of World War II, even counting the atomic bombings.

Meanwhile, US scientists successfully tested a nuclear weapon, and the US Army Air Force's 509th Composite Group was tasked with dropping them. Various cities were considered as targets; Hiroshima was chosen both for its large stockpiles of military supplies and as the headquarters of Japan's Second General Army.

------

[*] Operation Downfall is the subject of my alternate history novel (with Douglas Niles) *MacArthur's War* (New York: Forge, 2007).

Colonel Paul Tibbets, commanding officer of the 509th, piloted the chosen bomber, the B-29 *Enola Gay* (named for his mother). Six other planes accompanied the flight, responsible for reconnaissance, measurement, and photography. They reached the target roughly six hours after takeoff, and at roughly 8:15 AM Hiroshima time, *Enola Gay* released its payload.

The explosion was the equivalent of 16,000 kilotons of TNT, and destroyed everything within a mile (1.6 km). Fires swept across another 4.4 square miles (11 km^2), with roughly30% of the population of Hiroshima (70-80,000 people) killed by the initial blast and firestorm. In the days, weeks, and months following, many more died either from wounds received in the blast or by radiation exposure.

Japan vowed to fight on, and on August 9, a second bomb was dropped on Nagasaki. More bombs were on the way; Manhattan Project director Leslie Groves expected to have a third ready for August 19, three more in September, and three more in October. On August 14, however, before the third could be readied, the Shōwa Emperor[†] announced Japan's unconditional surrender.

[†] When Prince Hirohito became Emperor of Japan, by tradition he gave up his personal name, and was then known only as the Emperor. His reign was officially known as the Shōwa era (the "era of enlightened peace") and upon his death he is now known as the Shōwa Emperor.

The Hiroshima Peace Memorial is centered on the Prefectural
Industrial Promotional Hall, the closest surviving building to the site
of the detonation. It is known as the Genbaku Dome, part of the
Hiroshima Peace Memorial Park (Photo: US Department of Energy)

The B-29 *Enola Gay*, which dropped the bomb on Hiroshima, can
be seen at the Smithsonian Institution's National Air and Space
Museum's Steven F. Udvar-Hazy Center in Chantilly, Virginia

Cover Story
Curiosity Lands on Mars (2012)

On August 6, 2012, the NASA rover *Curiosity* landed on the surface of Mars as part of the Mars Science Laboratory Mission. Roughly the size of a car, the rover was tasked with studying Martian climate and geology, with particular focus on signs of life, water, and the potential for human survival.

The mission was planned to last for two years, but the *Curiosity* has (at the time of writing) passed its fifth anniversary and continues to operate. It has traveled nearly 11 miles (17 km) in its research.

Launched from Cape Canaveral on November 26, 2011, it took more than eight months to cover the roughly 350 million miles (560 million kilometers) from Earth to the Red Planet. The rover weighed nearly a ton and was powered by a radioisotope thermoelectric generator, which converts the heat from the decay of plutonium$_{238}$ into electricity.

The name Curiosity was selected by a nationwide student contents, with the winner being sixth-grader Clara Ma from Lenexa, Kansas. The landing site on Mars has been named Bradbury Landing in honor of science fiction writer Ray Bradbury.

A number of scientific discoveries and immense amounts of data have been produced by Curiosity. It has determined that Mars once had environmental conditions favorable for microbial life, an important step toward humanity's inevitable voyage to our neighboring planet.

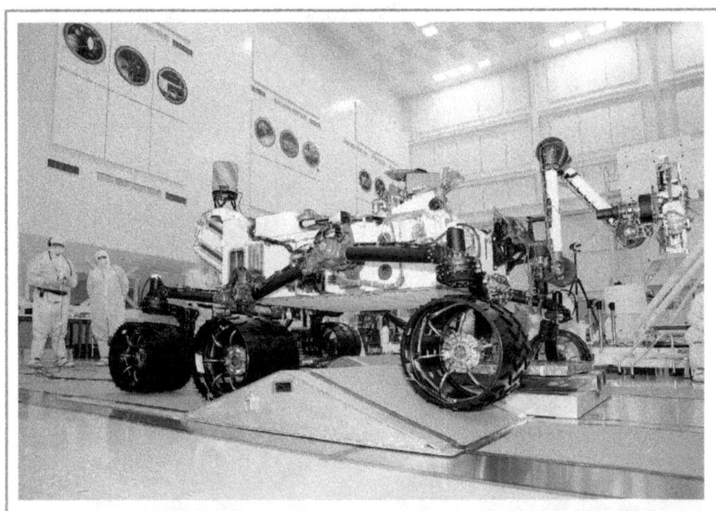

The *Curiosity* rover on Earth, showing its relative size

Artist conception of *Curiosity* at work

Francis II, by Friedrich von Amerling

More August 6 Events

From the creation of great works of engineering and art, to devastating wars and natural disasters, thousands of years of history have left their mark on each and every day of the year. Here are some important events that occurred on August 6. (Illustrated items are shaded.)

1806 — After his defeat by Napoleon at the Battle of Austerlitz, Emperor Francis II dissolves the **Holy Roman Empire**, which traced its origins back to the coronation of Charlemagne more than a thousand years earlier.

1819 — **Norwich University**, the oldest of the six senior military colleges and the "birthplace of ROTC" is founded.

1890 — Convicted murderer William Kemmler is the first person in the world legally **executed by electric chair.**

1914 — World War I's **First Battle of the Atlantic** begins when ten German U-boats set out to attack Royal Navy warships in the first submarine war patrols in history.

1926 — American Olympic swimming champion Gertrude Ederle becomes the **first woman to swim across the English Channel**. *(Photo page 16.)*

Gertrude Ederle swims the English Channel (Photo: George Grantham Bain)

1930 — In one of the most famous missing persons cases of the 20th century, **Judge Joseph Crater vanishes** after leaving a restaurant in New York. The case has never been solved.

1965 — US President Lyndon B. Johnson signs the landmark **Voting Rights Act** of 1965, prohibiting racial discrimination in voting.

1996 — The punk rock group **the Ramones** play their final concert at the Hollywood Palace.

The Ramones (left to right: Johnny Ramone, Tommy Ramone (back), Joey Ramone, and Dee Dee Ramone (Photo: Plismo, CC BY-SA 3.0)

Quote of the Day

"Only rarely can we repay those people who helped us, but we can pass that help along to others."

Lucille Ball, comedianne and actress
born August 6, 1911

Births
and
Deaths

THEICA
AC—
MAGNA

August 6

Lucille Ball, right, with husband and co-star Desi Arnaz in a 1956 episode of *I Love Lucy*. Lucille Ball was born August 6, 1911

Notable August 6 People

With the current world population at about seven billion people, on average about 19 million people also celebrate their birthdays on August 6 — and that isn't counting millions and millions who came before! No matter when you were born, you share your birthday with many special people whose accomplishments (and occasionally embarrassments) have been noted as part of history.

In this section, you'll meet fascinating people who share your birthday. They're organized by what they're famous for, and then in reverse chronological order from most recent to earliest. Those who are shown in photographs or artwork have a box around them. We don't have photos of everyone, so please forgive us if your favorite person is missing.

Some of these people you've heard of, others will be new to you, but they all make up an important part of the reason that August 6 is a truly special day!

Campbell's Soup Cans, by Andy Warhol (Photo: Maurizio Pesce, CC BY-SA 2.0)

Who Was Born on August 6?

Art

Andy Warhol, leading figure in the "pop art" movement. His best known works include *Campbell's Soup Cans* and *Marilyn Diptych;* coined the expression "15 minutes of fame." *(1928)*

Business

Sir Freddy Laker, English entrepreneur who founded the first "no frills" airline, Laker Airways. *(1922)*

Crime and Punishment

Kevin Mitnick, served five years in prison in a controversial case of computer hacking; subsequently became a computer security consultant. Subject of the 2000 film *Track Down.* *(1963)*

Charles Ingram, convicted for cheating to win the £1,000,000 jackpot on the British edition of the game show *Who Wants to Be a Millionaire? (1963)*

Samuel Bowers, white supremacist who-founded the White Knights of the Ku Klux Klan; convicted of the 1964 murders of three civil rights activists in Mississippi and the 1966 murder of civil rights leader Vernon Dahmer. *(1924)*

Dutch Schultz, mobster in the 1920s and 1930s, active in bootlegging and the numbers racket. *(1902)*

Dutch Schultz (mugshot)

Literature and Journalism

Paolo Bacigalupi, science fiction and fantasy writer whose work has won the Hugo, Nebula, and Theodore Sturgeon Awards; best known works include *The Windup Girl* and *Ship Breaker*. *(1972)*

Piers Anthony, science fiction and fantasy author best known for his long-running novel series *Xanth*. *(1934)*

Elisabeth Beresford, children's book author best known for creating The Wombles. *(1926)*

Barbara Cooney, children's book author and illustrator who won Caldecott Medals for her books *Chanticleer and the Fox* and *Ox-Cart Man. (1917)*

Richard Hofstadter, historian and public intellectual who received two Pulitzer Prizes for his work. *(1916)*

Louella Parsons, wrote the first gossip column for an American newspaper and became the first Hollywood columnist for William Randolph Hearst;s newspapers. Known as the Queen of Hollywood, her columns appeared in 400 newspapers with a readership of 20 million. *(1881)*

Louella Parsons

Charles Fort, researcher and writer who specialized in "anomalous phenomena," things that fall outside current understanding. Authored numerous books and inspired "Forteans," who continue his inquiries into unexplained and paranormal matters. *(1874)*

Alfred, Lord Tennyson, Poet Laureate of Great Britain during the reign of Queen Victoria, best known for "The Charge of the Light Brigade." *(1809)*

Alfred, Lord Tennyson (Photo: Julia Margaret Cameron)

Military

George Kenney, US Army Air Force general who commanded allied air forces in the Southwest Pacific Area theater of World War II; first commander of the Strategic Air Command (SAC). *(1889)*

Music

Geri Halliwell, singer-songwriter best known as Ginger Spice in the girl group the Spice Girls. *(1972)*

Geri Halliwell (Photo: Max Village, CC BY-SA 4.0)

Elliott Smith, singer-songwriter whose 1997 song "Miss Misery" from *Good Will Hunting* was nominated for a Best Original Song Oscar. *(1969)*

Randy DeBarge, singer and guitarist best known as a member of the Motown family group DeBarge. *(1958)*

Charlie Haden, jazz double bass player and composer first known as an original member of the Ornette Coleman Quartet; known for revolutionizing the harmonic concept of bass playing in jazz. *(1937)*

Baden Powell, celebrated Brazilian guitarist and composer known for works in bossa nova, samba, jazz, and música popular brasileira. *(1937)*

Norman Granz, known as the most successful impressario in jazz history; founded the labels Clef, Norgran, Down Home, Verve, and Pablo. *(1918)*

Performing Arts

Melissa George, actress who appeared in *Mulholland Drive*, *The Amityville Horror* (2005), and other films, as well as TV series *Grey's Anatomy* and *Lie to Me*. *(1976)*

Soleil Moon Frye, actress best known for playing the title role in the sitcom *Punky Brewster*. *(1976)*

Vera Farminga, actress nominated for a Best Supporting Actress Oscar for the 2009 film *Up in the Air*; also known for roles in *Bates Motel* and *The Conjuring* film series. *(1973)*

Cast of *The Bob Newhart Show.* Standing from left, Bill Daily, Marcia Wallace, **Peter Bonerz** (page 28). Seated, Bob Newhart, Suzanne Pleshette

M. Night Shyamalan, filmmaker known for supernatural plots and surprise endings, including 1999's *The Sixth Sense. (1970)*

Michelle Yeoh, actress known for roles in the James Bond film *Tomorrow Never Dies; Crouching Tiger, Hidden Dragon;* and *Memoirs of a Geisha. (1962)*

Catherine Hicks, known for roles in *7th Heaven, Ryan's Hope,* and *Star Trek IV: The Voyage Home. (1951)*

Dorian Harewood, actor known for roles in the ABC miniseries *Roots: The Next Generation,*the films *Full Metal Jacket* and *The Jesse Owens Story,* and the television series *I'll Fly Away. (1950)*

Louise Sorel, actress best known for roles on the daytime dramas *Santa Barbara, One Life to Live,* and *Days of Our Lives. (1940)*

Peter Bonerz, actor best known for playing Dr. Jerry Robinson on the sitcom *The Bob Newhart Show. (1938) (Photo page 27.)*

Paul Bartel, wrote, directed, and starred in the 1982 black comedy *Eating Raoul. (1938)*

Barbara Windsor, English actress known for roles in the *Carry On* film series and the soap opera *EastEnders. (1937)*

Michael Deeley, produced such films as *The Italian Job, The Deer Hunter,* and *Blade Runner. (1932)*

Abbey Lincoln, jazz vocalist and actress best known for roles in *The Girl Can't Help It, For Love of Ivy,* and *Mo' Better Blues. (1930)*

Frank Finlay, English actor whose best known roles include the villain in 1973's *Shaft in Africa,* and Porthos in Richard Lester's 1973 film *The Three Musketeers* and its sequel. *(1926)*

Ella Raines, actress and World War II pin-up girl whose films include *Phantom Lady* and *Hail the Conquering Hero;* starred in the 1950s television series *Janet Dean, Registered Nurse. (1920)*

Ella Raines (Photo: Walter Sanders)

Selma Diamond, comic actress and television writer best known for playing the character Selma Hacker on the sitcom *Night Court*; wrote for Sid Caesar's groundbreaking *Your Show of Shows* and is thought to have been the inspiration for the character Sally Rogers on *The Dick Van Dyke Show*. *(1920)*

Robert Mitchum, known for his antihero and film noir roles in such films as *The Night of the Hunter* and *Cape Fear*; listed as one of the greatest stars of classic American cinema by the American Film Institute. *(1917)*

Lucille Ball, actress, comedienne, and producer best known for the sitcom *I Love Lucy* and its later spinoffs; first woman to run a major television studio. Received a Lifetime Achievement Award from the Kennedy Center Honors and inducted into the Television Hall of Fame. *(1911) (Photo page 18.)*

Charles Crichton, filmmaker nominated for two Academy Awards (Best Director and Best Original Screenplay) for his 1988 film *A Fish Called Wanda*. *(1910)*

Hoot Gibson, rodeo champion and cowboy film star in the silent film era and early talkies. *(1892) (Photo page 32.)*

Leo Carrillo, actor best known for playing Pancho in the *The Cisco Kid* films and television series. *(1880) (Photo page 32.)*

Robert Mitchum (right) with Faith Domergue in *Where Danger Lives* (RKO, 1950)

Hoot Gibson in *A Hero on Horseback* (1927)

Autographed photo of Leo Carrillo as Pancho from *The Cisco Kid*

Record Setters

Anna Haining Bates, Canadian giantess who reached a height of 7 feet, 11.5 inches (2.43 meters), and who gave birth to the largest newborn ever recorded, 23 lbs., 9 oz. *(1846)*

Science and Mathematics

Sir Alexander Fleming, Scottish researcher best known for the discovery of penicillin, for which he shared the 1945 Nobel Prize in Physiology or Medicine. *(1881)*

William Hyde Wollaston, English scientist who discovered the chemical elements palladium and rhodium, and developed a method of processing platinum ore into malleable ingots. *(1766)*

Johann Bernoulli, member of the noted Bernoulli family of Swiss mathematicians, known for his contributions to the development of infinitesimal calculus. Bernoulli's rule and Bernoulli's identity are named for him. *(1667[‡])*

[‡] Johann Bernoulli was born when the "Old Style" Julian calendar was still in effect, and died under the "New Style" Gregorian calendar. His date of birth is normally written as August 6, 1677 [O. S. July 27]. For a discussion on the difference between the Julian and Gregorian calendars, see "What Day of the Week is August 6?"

Sports

Garrett Weber-Gale, American competition swimmer who won two Olympic gold medals in the 2008 Tokyo games. *(1985)*

Max Kellerman, sports television personality known as co-host of the ESPN talk show *SportsNation*. *(1963)*

Mike Greenberg, television anchor and host known for ESPN's *SportsCenter* and the radio show *Mike & Mike*. *(1967)*

David Robinson, basketball center for the San Antonio Spurs and two-time Olympic gold medalist with the US team; member of the Naismith Memorial Basketball Hall of Fame; only graduate of the US Naval Academy to play in the NBA. *(1965)*

Ray Culp, pitcher for the Phillies, Cubs, and Red Sox in a ten-year career in Major League Baseball. *(1941)*

Clem Labine, relief pitcher who helped lead the Dodgers to their first World Series title; set a National League record for career saves in 1958. *(1926)*

Pauline Betz, World No. 1 American tennis player who won five Grand Slam titles; member of the International Tennis Hall of Fame and the ITA Women's Collegiate Tennis Hall of Fame. *(1919)* *(Photo page 36.)*

David Robinson (with baskeball) at the 1992 Olympic Games
(Photo: Ken Hackman/USAF)

 Michael Dobson

Pauline Betz (1949 advertisement for Camel cigarettes)

James Henry Greathead

Helen Jacobs, World No. 1 American tennis player who won nine Grand Slam titles. Served as a commander in US Navy intelligence during World War II, one of only five women to achieve that rank. Member of the International Tennis Hall of Fame and the National Gay and Lesbian Sports Hall of Fame *(1908)*

Henry Iba, basketball coach for Oklahoma State University, won two NCAA Division I championships and two Olympic gold medals for coaching the US men's national basketball team; member of the Naismith Memorial Basketball Hall of Fame and the National Collegiate Basketball Hall of Fame. *(1904)*

Technology and Engineering

Rajendra Singh, conservationist known as the "waterman of India" for his pioneering work in water harvesting and water management; winner of the Ramon Magsaysay Award and the Stockholm Water Prize. *(1959)*

Cecil Howard Green, geophysicist who become one of the founders of Texas Instruments. *(1900)*

James Henry Greathead, civil engineer and inventor known for his work on the London Underground, and the reason it is known as "the tube." *(1844)*

Self Portrait, Diego Velázquez

Who Died on August 6?

Art and Architecture

Robert Hughes, art critic best known as creator and host of the 1980 documentary series on modern art, *The Shock of the New. (1973)*

Edward Durell Stone, architect whose best known works include Radio City Music Hall, the Kennedy Center, and New York's Museum of Modern Art. *(1978)*

Diego Velázquez, leading figure in the Spanish Golden Age of painting, influenced numerous modern realist and impressionist painters, including Manet, Picasso, and Dalí. *(1660)*

Radio City Music Hall, designed by **Edward Durell Stone**. (Photo: Kenny Louie, CC BY-SA 2.0)

Business

Robert Spear Hudson, English businessman who developed the first successful dry soap powder. *(1884)*

Advertisement for Hudson's Dry Soap, developed by **Robert Spear Hudson** (Courtesy Wellcome Images, CC BY-SA 4.0)

Government and Politics

Fulgencio Batista, president of Cuba and leader of a 1952 military coup; overthrown by Fidel Castro during the Cuban Revolution. *(1973)*

Literature and Journalism

Harry Reasoner, television journalist best known as a founder of the long-running news series *60 Minutes. (1991)*

Fulgencio Batista in front of a map showing the location of Fidel
Castro's rebel forces

Ben Jonson, English playwright and poet whose best
known works include *Every Man in His Humour;
Volpone, or The Fox;* and *Bartholomew Fair;* generally
regarded as the second-most important Jacobean era
playwright after Shakespeare. *(1637) (Portrait page 42.)*

Ben Jonson, after Abraham van Blijenberch

Military

Richard Bong, highest-scoring American flying ace in World War II, credited with shooting down 40 Japanese aircraft; received the Medal of Honor. *(1945)*

Richard Bong

Music

Marvin Hamlisch, musician best known for "The Entertainer," the theme song for the film *The Sting*, as well as "The Way We Were," and "Nobody Does It Better." One of only two people to win an Emmy, a Grammy, an Oscar, a Tony (EGOT), and a Pulitzer Prize. *(2012)*

Martin Hamlisch receiving three Academy Awards at the 1974 Oscars. From left to right, Donald O'Connor, Debbie Reynolds, **Marvin Hamlisch,** and Cher Bono (Credit: Associated Press)

Rick James, funk and soul artist whose best known hit was 1981's "Super Freak." *(2004)*

Bix Beiderbecke, jazz cornetist whose short and influential life was the subject of the 1938 novel and 1950 film *Young Man With a Horn*. His best known songs include "Way Down Yonder in New Orleans," "In a Mist," and "For No Reason at All in C." *(1931)* *(Photo page 44.)*

Performing Arts

John Hughes, filmmaker known for such films as *Sixteen Candles, The Breakfast Club, Pretty in Pink,* and *Home Alone. (2009)*

Bix Beiderbecke with his band The Wolverines. Beiderbeck is seated, fourth from the left.

Cedric Hardwicke, stage and screen actor known for various classical roles, as well as for the 1939 adaptation of *The Hunchback of Notre Dame* and the 1942 film *The Ghost of Frankenstein. (1964)*

Preston Sturges, Academy Award-winning filmmaker best known for his screwball comedies, including *The Great McGinty, The Lady Eve, Sullivan's Travels, The Miracle of Morgan Creek,* and many others. *(1959)*

Religion

Pope Paul VI, pope of the Catholic Church from 1963 to his death in 1978. *(1978)*

James Springer White, co-founder of the Seventh-Day Adventist Church. *(1881)*

John Mason Neil, priest and hymn-writer whose best-known works include "Good Christian Men, Rejoice," "Good King Wenceslas," and "O Come, O Come Emmanuel." *(1866)*

Saint Dominic, founded the *Ordo Praedicatorium,* commonly known as the Dominican Order; patron saint of astronomers. *(1221)*

Saint Dominic in Prayer, by El Greco (c. 1605)

Science

Feodor Lynen, shared the 1964 Nobel Prize in Physiology or Medicine for discoveries involving the mechanism and regulation of cholesterol. *(1979)*

Georg Richmann, German physicist who first proved thunder clouds contain electric charge; killed by lightning while experimenting, becoming the first person in history to die while conducting electrical experiments. *(1753)*

Death of Georg Wilhelm Richmann

Sports

Betty Cuthbert, Australian athlete who won four Olympic gold medals in track events at the 1956 and 1964 games. *(2017)*

Mava Lee Thomas, infielder and catcher for the All-American Girls Professional Baseball League. *(2013)*

Tony Lazzeri, second baseman best known as part of the 1920s "Murderers' Row" lineup of the New York Yankees; member of the Baseball Hall of Fame. *(1946)*

1933 Goudey baseball card of Tony Lazzeri

Quote of the Day

"The fate of all explanation is to close one door only to have another fly wide open."

Charles Fort, researcher of
strange phenomena
born August 6, 1874

51

Pigeon Point Lighthouse, California (Photo © 2016 Frank Schulenberg, CC BY-SA 4.0) — for **National Lighthouse Day**

August 6 Events

If you're looking for a reason to take your special day off, you should know that every single day is a holiday somewhere in the world! Here's some of what you can celebrate on August 6!

General Events

Children's Day (Tuvalu)
The Polynesian island nation of Tuvalu celebrates Children's Day each August 6.

Dia de la Patria (Bolivia)
The South American nation of Bolivia celebrates the declaration of its independence from Spain, which took place August 6, 1825.

Independence Day (Jamaica)
The Caribbean nation of Jamaica celebrates the granting of its independence from the United Kingdom on August 6, 1962.

National Lighthouse Day (US)
The United States Congress first approved legislation for lighthouses, beacons, and other safety measures on August 6, 1789.

Peace Memorial Ceremony (Hiroshima, Japan)
Each year, the city of Hiroshima holds a Peace Memorial Ceremony for the victims of the atomic bombing of that city on August 6, 1945, and to pray for the realization of lasting world peace.

Railway Troops Day (День железнодорожных войск) (Russia)

Railway troops are soldiers who are also railway engineers. Their mission is to build, repair, operate, and sometimes destroy vital railroad infrastructure in times of war. The Russian Railway Troops, the oldest such force in the world, celebrate their founding on August 6, 1851.

Soldiers meet an incoming train — for **Railway Troops Day**

Food Days

In the United States, almost every day of the year is dedicated to a particular food. (Some other countries also have official food days, but only in America is there one every single day!) Sponsored by manufacturers, retailers, farmers, or simply fans, these days are often proclaimed by the President, Congress, state governors, or mayors. Given that there are more different foods than days of the year, some days honor more than one kind of food!

In the US, August 6 is **National Root Beer Float Day.**

A soda jerk serves a root beer float — for **National Root Beer Float Day** (Photo: Alan Fisher, New York *World-Telegram and Sun*)

Root beer, a soft drink traditionally made from sassafras or sarsaparilla, evolved from traditional Native American beverages, and frequently contained alcohol.

Small batches of modern root beer, mixing the syrup with soda water, first appeared in the 1850s, but the first successful commercial version was Hires Root Beer, made by pharmacist Charles Elmer Hires and first shown to the public at the 1876 Philadelphia Centennial Exposition. Hires, a teetotaler, wanted to call it "root tea," but went with "root beer" instead, hoping to appeal to Pennsylvania coal miners.

A root beer float (also called a "black cow" or "brown cow") is usually made with root beer and vanilla ice cream.

The first ice cream float was made in 1874 by Robert McCay Green, who ran out of ice for the flavored drinks he was selling and substituted ice cream. (Some people claim to have done it earlier, but Green's version was the one that caught on.)

He was so proud of his accomplishment that he had the words "Originator of the Ice Cream Soda" engraved on his tombstone.

In some jurisdictions, ice cream floats were banned on holy days, so a sodaless version was created. These were called ice cream sundaes, because they were sold on "soda's day of rest."

A 19th century advertisement for Hires Root Beer — for **National Root Beer Float Day**

If August 6 falls on the first Thursday, it's also **India Pale Ale Beer Day,** and if it's the first Friday, it's **International Beer Day.** The day after International Beer Day, which can also fall on August 6, is **International Hangover Day.** If you don't like beer, there's always **Mead Day,** held on the first Saturday.

If it's the first Friday, it's **Homemade Pie Day.** Homemade pie goes well with ice cream. If it's the first Sunday, it's **National Mustard Day.** Hopefully you've already eaten all the pie.

Christmas Pie, by William Henry Hunt — for **Homemade Pie Day**

Food Months

In addition, the entire month of August is used to celebrate numerous foods. Here's a list of what to eat in the month of August!

- National Catfish Month
- National Goat Cheese Month
- National Panini Month
- National Peach Month
- National Sandwich Month

August is also **Family Meals Month**, if you're willing to share that homemade pie.

Jar of Peaches, by Claude Monet — for **National Peach Month**

Religious Feast Days and Holidays

Feast of the Transfiguration of Jesus (Christianity)

A number of Christian communities celebrate the Feast of the Transfiguration, observed on August 6. "Old Calendrist" Orthodox churches that use the Julian calendar for liturgical purposes celebrate it on August 19§.

Saint Days

Each day in the year is considered a feast day for one or more saints. They are somewhat different in western Christianity (Catholicism and many forms of Protestantism) and in eastern (Orthodox) Christianity.

In *Western Christianity*, August 6 is the feast day of Saints Hormisdas, Justus and Pastor, and the Blessed Anna Maria Rubatto.

In *Eastern Orthodox Christianity*, it is also the commemoration of Saints Hardulf, Gezelin, Stephen of Cardeña, Theoctistus, and Daniel Kushnir Mlievsky-Cherkasky. (These saints are honored on July 24 by "Old Calendrists.")

---

§ See "What Day of the Week is August 6?" for more on the differences between the Julian and Gregorian calendars.

Transfiguration, by Raphael — for **Feast of the Transfiguration**

Honorary Months and Moveable Celebrations

Presidents, Congresses, and nations around the world issue proclamations recognizing particular months to honor certain causes. If not otherwise specified, all months are US. Here are some honorary designations for August.

- American Adventures Month
- American Artists Appreciation Month
- American Indian Heritage Month
- Audio Appreciation Month
- Bystander Awareness Month
- Children's Eye Health and Safety Month
- Child Support Awareness Month
- National Children's Vision and Learning Month
- Digestive Tract Paralysis (DTP) Month
- Get Ready for Kindergarten Month
- Month of Philippine Languages (Philippines)
- National Back to School Month
- National Black Business Month
- National Breastfeeding Month
- National Immunization Awareness Month
- National Lawn Games Month
- National Minority Donor Awareness Month
- National Water Quality Month
- Neurosurgery Outreach Month
- Psoriasis Awareness Month
- Spinal Muscular Atrophy Awareness Month
- Tomboy Tools Month
- What Will Be Your Legacy Month
- Win with Civility Month

August is **Get Ready for Kindergarten Month**! This 1943 photograph is from a nursery school operated for women working in the war effort. (Photo: Marjory Collins for the Farm Security Administration, Office of War Information)

Moveable and Multi-Day Events

Some events take place over a specific week or time period. Some events occur on different days each year (such as "fourth Saturday of a month"). These events sometimes take place on or include August 6. All are US unless otherwise specified.

Week-Long Celebrations

- Psychic Week, first full week in August
- International Assistance Dog Week, first week in August

Movable Events

- American Family Day, first Sunday
- Assistance Dog Day, Monday of International Assistance Dog Week
- Friendship Day, first Sunday
- National Disc Golf Day, first Saturday
- National Doll Day, first Sunday
- National Fresh Breath Day, first Sunday
- National Kids' Day, first Sunday
- National Psychic Day, Monday of Psychic Week
- Sister's Day, first Sunday
- Tomboy Tools Day, first Friday
- Twins Day, first full weekend

Just for Fun

Anybody can make up a holiday, and many people do! While none of these are officially recognized and some may come and go, here are a few more holidays for August 6.

- Kadooment Day (Barbados), a carnival-type festival celebrated on the first Monday of August
- Wiggle Your Toes Day

A trading card of a girl and her doll — for **National Doll Day**

Quote of the Day

"Make haste slowly."

Augustus, first emperor of Rome
and namesake of the month of August

About
the
Month
of

August

"August," from the *Brevarium Grimani* by Simon Bening (c.1510)

August: The Eighth Month

In the parching August wind,
Cornfields bow the head,
Sheltered in round valley depths,
On low hills outspread.
  — *"A Year's Windfalls," Christina G. Rossetti*

In ancient Rome, the month we know as August was originally known as *Sextilis*, meaning sixth. That's because the Roman calendar of the time had March as the first month of the year. It originally had only 29 days, but in his great calendar reform in 45 BCE, Julius Caesar added two days to the month. In 8 BCE, the month was renamed August in honor of Augustus, first emperor of Rome.

It's often claimed that Augustus stole one of February's days to add to his month, but the month already had 31 days long before Augustus became emperor. Augustus chose the month because it was the time of year in which he had accomplished some of his greatest triumphs, including the conquest of Egypt.

In both the Julian and Gregorian calendars, August is the eighth month of the year. It's one of seven months that have 31 days. During leap years, August and February start on the same day of the week; in non-leap years years, no month begins on the same day of the week as August. However, August and November always end on the same day of the week, regardless of the type of year.

In the Northern Hemisphere, August is a summer month, and in many European countries, the holiday month for most workers. In the Southern Hemisphere, August is the equivalent to February, deep in winter. No matter which hemisphere, August is a good month to spot a meteor; the Perseid Meteor Shower always takes place during the month.

August is also the month in the US that has the highest birthrate.

August in Other Cultures

The month of August has different names in different languages. Some nations use calendars other than the Gregorian, and their months may overlap with June. In lunar-based calendars, such as Islam, months move through the seasons. Still, many languages often have a word for August itself.

Albanian: Gusht

Arabic (Egypt, Sudan, Yemen): يونأغسطس (Aġustus)

Arabic (Levant): حزيراآب ('āb)

Arabic (Libya): الصهانيبال (hānībāl)

Arabic (Algeria and Tunisia): جوأوت (Ūt)

Arabic (Morocco): غشت (ġušt)

Azerbaijani: Avqust

Basque: Abuztu

Chinese: 八月 (Cantonese: baatyuht; Mandarin: bāyuè; Taiwanese: peh-goeh)

Croatian: Kolovoz

Czech: Srpen

Finnish: Elokuu

French: Août

German (Swiss): Auguscht (in other German dialects, it's just "August.")

Greek: Αύγουστος (Aúgoustos)

Hebrew: אוגוסט (âvgûst)

Hindi: अगस्त (agast)

Hungarian: Augusztus

Irish (Gaelic): Lúnasa mí Lúnasa

Italian: Agosto

Japanese (traditional calendar): 九月 (kugatsu), 長月 (nagatsuki)

Korean: 팔월 (palweol)

Lithuanian: Rugpjūtis

Maori: Hereturikōkā

Old English: Wēodmōnaþ

Polish: Sierpień

Russian: август (Avgust)

Sesotho: Phato

Spanish and Portuguese: Agosto

Swahili: Agosti

Thai: Singhakhom

Vietnamese: 腑儳 (tháng tám)

Welsh: Awst

Yiddish: אויגוסט (oygust)

Zulu: uAgasti

August Sayings and Superstitions

Here are some sayings and superstitions associated with the month of August.

General Supersitions

"Agosto, mês do desgosto," or "August, the month of sorrow and grief." (Brazil)

"If a cold August follows a hot July/It foretells a winter hard and dry." (Farming)

If thunderstorms occur in early August, they will continue for the rest of the month.

Don't sail on the second Monday in August, because it was the day the ancient kingdoms of Sodom and Gomorrah were destroyed. (Old seafaring superstition)

If you bathe at midnight on August 1 (Lammas Day) in Lockmaur, Sutherlandshire, you'll be cured of all bodily ailments, but you're expected to repay the Spirit of the Lake with coin. (Scotland)

Wedding Supersitions

"August, better have waited." (Western Kentucky)

"An August bride will be agreeable, And practical as well."

"Married in August's heat and drowse/Lover and friend in your chosen spouse."

"Whoever wed in August be, many a change is sure to see."

The following days in August are considered auspicious for weddings: August 2, 11, 18, 20 and 30.

As for which day of the week to get married, that's easy.

Monday for health, Tuesday for wealth,
Wednesday best of all, Thursday for losses,
Friday for crosses, Saturday for no luck at all.

A Regency wedding proposal

August Symbols

Birthstone: Peridot or sardonyx.

Peridot

Sardonyx (The ancient Cup of the Ptolemies, probably made in
Alexandria, Egypt, in the 1st Century CE)

Birth Flowers: Poppy or Gladiolus, both symbolizing strength of character, love, marriage, and family.

Vase with Cornflowers and Poppies, by Vincent van Gogh

Vase with Red Gladioli, by Vincent van Gogh

"August," by Eugène Grasset

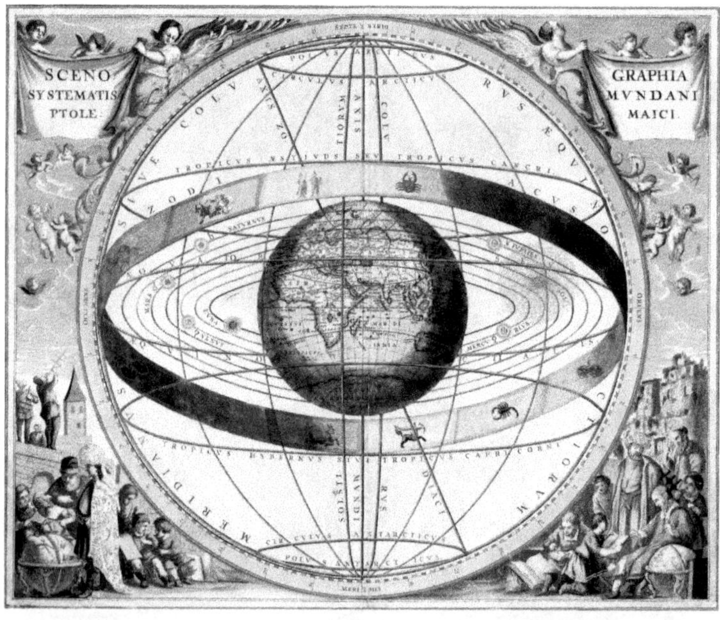

Scenography of the Ptolemaic Cosmography, by Johannes van Loon, based on Andreas Cellarius's *Harmonia Macrocosmica,* 1660

August 6 Zodiac Signs

From the perspective of someone on Earth, the Sun appears to move through the sky throughout the year, along a path astronomers call the *ecliptic plane*. The ecliptic plane is divided into twelve constellations, known as the zodiac, based on traditionally observed patterns of stars. On your birthday, you can't see your constellation, because it's in the daytime sky.

The zodiac was first developed by Babylonian astronomers about 2,500 years ago. Because they were unaware that the Earth wobbles like a spinning top (known as *precession*), they didn't make allowance for the fact that the Sun's path through the zodiac changes over time.

That means there are now two sets of dates for your birth sign. The *tropical dates* are the original Babylonian dates; the *sidereal dates* tell you where the Sun actually appears as it moves along its annual path.

For August 6, the tropical sign is **Leo** and the sidereal sign is **Cancer.**

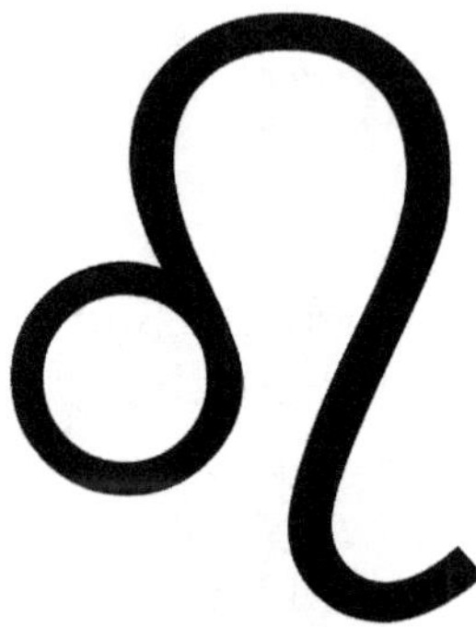

Leo

Tropical July 23 to August 22
Sidereal August 16 to September 15

Leo is one of the earliest recognizable constellations, with its stars forming a sickle or backward question mark. The Mesopotamians, the Persians, the Jews, and the Indians all had a name for the constellation that meant "lion." In Greek mythology, the Nemean lion was impervious to any weapons, but the hero Hercules nevertheless defeated it.

In astrology, Leo is a fire sign, suggesting that Leos are strong-willed and passionate. Leos are supposed to be compatible with Aquarius, Aries, and Sagittarius, but not with Gemini, Capricorn, or Pisces.

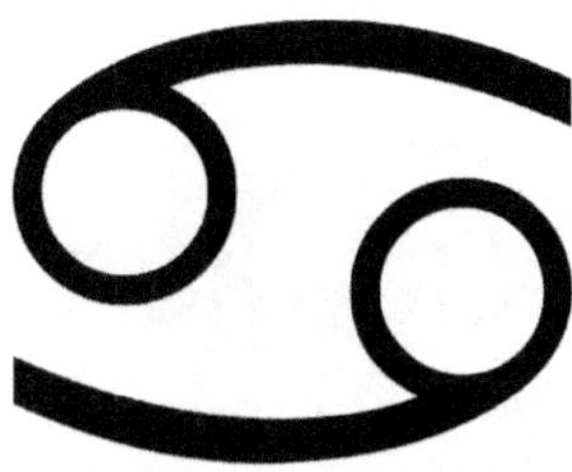

Cancer

Tropical June 21 to July 22
Sidereal July 16 to August 15

The Greek word for "crab" is Καρκινος (*Karkinos*), later Latinized as *carcinus*, which evolved into our word cancer. In Greek mythology, when Hercules was battling the Hydra, Zeus's wife Hera sent Karkinos to distract the hero, but Hercules kicked it with such force that it was thrown into the sky, becoming a constellation.

Because of the association with the disease, some astrologers refer to those born under the sign of Cancer as "moon children," because the ruling planet of Cancer is the Moon.

Cancers (or Moon Children) are supposed to be loyal, dependable, caring, and adaptable, but can also be moody, self-pitying, and oversensitive. Cancers are supposed to be particularly compatible with Scorpios, Piceans, and other Cancers.

Illustration by Edward Penfield

What Day of the Week is August 6?

On what day of the week does August 6 fall?

Surprisingly, this isn't an easy question. Because the calendar year is 365 days long (366 in leap years), it doesn't divide evenly by the seven days of the week.

Also, the Earth goes around the Sun in about 365-1/4 days, so a calendar tends to drift over time. That's why the same date falls on different weekdays in different years.

This is made even more complicated by a change in calendars that took place in 1582. Our modern calendar has its roots in ancient Rome, in a calendar reform conducted by Julius Caesar. Caesar commissioned mathematicians to attack the problem, and they came up with the idea of leap years, and thus standardized the calendar for centuries to come. This was called the Julian calendar.

Over time, however, the small errors in Caesar's calculation compounded. That's why Pope Gregory XIII commissioned the Gregorian calendar, used in most of the world today. Some countries converted in 1582, when the calendar was first developed; some converted later; other still haven't changed.

Gregorian and Julian aren't the only types of calendars. The Hebrew year, the Islamic year, and many other calendars are used in different parts of the world and among different people.

You can convert Gregorian dates to other calendars, including the Hebrew calendar, the Islamic calendar, and even the Mayan calendar by visiting the Fourmilab Calendar Converter at http://www.fourmilab.ch/documents/calendar/.

Chinese calendar systems are quite complex and have changed several times; a full discussion is far beyond the scope of this book. If you're interested, you can find information here: http://www.hermetic.ch/cal_stud/chinese_cal.htm.

On Names and Dates

Historians use "CE" (Common Era) and "BCE" (Before the Common Era) instead of the more common "AD" (Anno Domini, or Year of Our Lord) and "BC" (Before Christ), reflecting the fact that the year-numbering system established by the Gregorian calendar is used throughout the world in many countries not culturally Christian.

The CE/BCE designation dates back to at least 1708, and has been adopted as a standard by the United Nations and the Universal Postal Union. Because this series of books covers events and people of all nations and cultures, we use the CE/BCE terms.

The abbreviation "O.S." ("Old Style") and "N.S." ("New Style") on some dates refers to the fact that the Russian Empire (in particular) did not switch from the Julian to the Gregorian calendar at the same time as the rest of Europe, and therefore some figures and events have two dates.

Also, in the Julian calendar in England in the 16th century, the year began on March 25 rather than January 1. To avoid confusion with Gregorian dates, dates between January and March were often written using both years.

People and events whose original names are not in the Western alphabet have their native names (where possible) in the appropriate script shown in parenthesis. If you are using an e-reader to access an electronic version of this book, all characters don't always display on all devices.

A 50-year brass perpetual calendar.

Quote of the Day

"Time is an illusion, lunchtime doubly so."

Douglas Adams,
from *The Hitchhiker's Guide to the Galaxy*

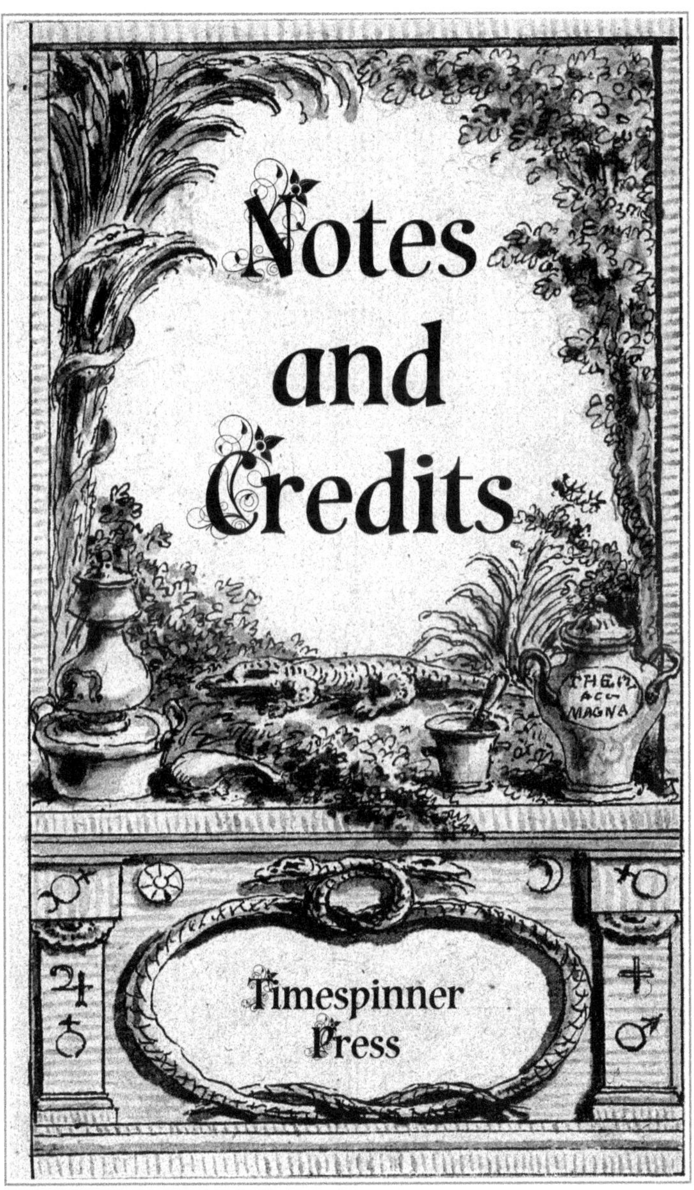

Notes
and
Credits
Timespinner
Press

Cartoon by John T. McCutcheon

Copyright, Credit, and Contact

Follow Us

Our blog "This Day in History" (http://
timespinnerpress.com/this-day-in-history/) features short
articles on events and people associated with each day, and
updates several times each week. Also subscribe to the
"Quote of the Day" at http://timespinnerpress.com/quote-
of-the-day/. You can get daily links by following us on
Facebook at TimespinnerPress, or on Twitter as
@sidewisethinker.

Contact Us

Find an error or a format problem? Want information about
the series, about us, or about when the volume for your
special day might be available? Please email us at
editor@timespinnerpress.com. (We also take requests if your
special day isn't yet complete. Please give us at least six
weeks' notice if possible.)

Sources

We owe a great debt to Wikipedia, which is our first stop for
research. We attempt to make independent confirmation of
all important dates and facts through a variety of other
sources.

Other sources we frequently use include the Library of
Congress; "on this day" listings from *Encyclopedia Britannica*,
the *New York Times*, and the BBC; Omniglot for the names of
months in other languages; *Chase's Calendar of Events*; and, of
course, the always essential Google.

All art and photographs are either in the public domain, used under a Creative Commons license, or with a "fair use" justification, and most frequently come from Wikimedia Commons and the Library of Congress Prints and Photographs Division.

Attribution is provided where possible, or as requested by the copyright owner, or when there is particular historical significance, listed below. For information about any particular illustration or photograph, please contact us.

Credits

1. The 2015 cover photograph of NASA's Mars rover *Curiosity* is in the public domain as a work created solely by NASA.

2. The illustration of the month of August used on the back cover is from the French Gothic illuminated manuscript *Les Très Riches Heures du duc de Berry* by the Limbourg Brothers, Jean Colombe, and an intermediate painter whose name is lost to history. It is in the public domain because its copyright has expired.

3. The box graphic used on the first page is from a 1916 pamphlet entitled "Divorce versus Democracy" authored by G. K. Chesterton, originally published in London by the Society of St. Peter and St. Paul. It is in the public domain in the US because it was published prior to 1923, and is in the public domain in all countries (including the country of origin) in which the copyright time is the author's life plus 70 years or less.

4. The graphic design for the section pages in this book is from a design originally created for a pharmacy label. It is courtesy of Wellcome Images (ICV No 11073, photo V0010813), and is used here under CC BY-SA 4.0.

5. The trade card "The Moon of Sturgeon August" by P. D. Beckwith was created circa 1909, and is in the public domain because its copyright has expired. It is from the Victorian Trade Cards Collection at Miami University Libraries (accession no. 1200).

6. The August 6, 1945 photograph of the mushroom cloud over Hiroshima was taken by Staff Sergeant George R. (Bob) Caron, tail gunner on the B-29 *Enola Gay*. It is in the public domain as a work created by an employee of the US government as part of that person's official duties.

7. The 2014 photograph of the Peace Dome in Hiroshima was taken by an employee of the US Department of Energy, and is in the public domain as a work created by an employee of the US government as part of that person's official duties.

8. The 1945 photograph of *Enola Gay* returning from the bombing of Hiroshima is in the public domain as a work created by an employee of the US government as part of that person's official duties.

9. The photograph of *Curiosity* on Earth is in the public domain as a work created solely by NASA.

10. The artist's conception of *Curiosity* at work on the surface of Mars is in the public domain as a work created solely by NASA.

11. The 1832 painting of Francis II by Friedrich von Amerling is in the public domain because its copyright has expired. It can be seen in the Schönbrunn Palace, Vienna, Austria.

12. The 1926 photograph of Gertrude Ederle by the Bain News Service is from the George Grantham Bain collection at the Library of Congress, digital ID ggbain.37118. According to the Library, there are no known copyright restrictions on this work.

13. The 1976 photograph of the Ramones in concert is copyright © Plismo, and is used here under CC BY-SA 3.0.

14. The 1956 publicity photograph from *I Love Lucy* is in the public domain because it was first published in the United States between 1923 and 1977 without a copyright notice. Traditionally, publicity photographs are not copyrighted because of the way in which they are intended to be used.

15. The 2013 photograph of Andy Warhol's Campbell's Soup Cans is copyright © Maurizio Pesce, and is used here under CC BY-SA 2.0.

16. The mug shot of Dutch Schultz is in the public domain as a work created by an employee of the US government as part of that person's official duties.

17. The 1937 publicity photograph of Louella Parsons is in the public domain because it was first published in the United States between 1923 and 1977 without a copyright notice.

18. The photograph of Alfred, Lord Tennyson, was taken between 1870 and 1879 by Julia Margaret Cameron. It is in the public domain because its copyright has expired.

19. The 2017 photograph of Geri Halliwell is copyright © Max Village, and is used here under CC BY-SA 4.0.

20. The 1977 publicity photograph from *The Bob Newhart Show* is in the public domain because it was first published in the United States between 1923 and 1977 without a copyright notice.

21. The front cover of the February 28, 1944, issue of *Life* magazine is in the public domain because it was published in the United States between 1923 and 1963 and although there may or may not have been a copyright notice, the copyright was not renewed.

22. The 1950 publicity photograph from *Where Danger Lives* is in the public domain because it was first published in the United States between 1923 and 1977 without a copyright notice.

23. The lobby card from the 1927 film *A Hero on Horseback* is in the public domain because it was first published in the United States between 1923 and 1977 without a copyright notice.

24. The pre-1968 publicity photo from *The Cisco Kid* is in the public domain because it was first published in the United States between 1923 and 1977 without a copyright notice.

25. The 1992 photograph of David Robinson at the Olympic Games is by Ken Hackman, USAF (VIRIN JCCC92080016). It is in the public domain as a work created by an employee of the US government as part of that person's official duties.

26. The 1949 advertisement for Camel cigarettes is in the public domain because it was first published in the United States

between 1923 and 1977 without a copyright notice. The image has been cropped.

27. The photograph of James Henry Greathead was taken prior to 1896 and is in the public domain because its copyright has expired.

28. The self portrait of Diego Velázquez was created prior to 1660, and is in the public domain because its copyright has expired. It is in the Museum of John Paul II Collection (Porczyński Gallery), Warsaw, Poland.

29. The 2008 photograph of Radio City Music Hall is copyright © Kenny Louie, and is used here under CC BY-SA 2.0.

30. The advertisement for Hudson's Soap is courtesy Wellcome Images (GC EPH169, Photo L0069078), who has made the image available under CC BY-SA 4.0.

31. The 1957 photograph of Fulgencio Batista is in the public domain because it was first published in Cuba without compliance with US copyright formalities prior to February 20, 1972. It appeared in *Life* magazine in the US in March 1957.

32. The painting of Ben Jonson after Abraham van Blijenberch is in the public domain because its copyright has expired. The original is form the collection of the National Portrait Gallery, London, NPG 363.

33. The US Army Air Force World War II era photograph of Richard Bong is in the public domain as a work created by an employee of the US government as part of that person's official duties.

34. The 1974 Associated Press photo of the Oscars is in the public domain because it was first published in the United States between 1923 and 1977 without a copyright notice.

35. The 1924 photograph of the Wolverines is in the public domain because it was first published in the United States between 1923 and 1977 without a copyright notice.

36. The painting *Saint Dominic in Prayer* by El Greco was created circa 1605, and is in the public domain because its copyright has expired. It is in the collection of the Museum of Fine Arts, Boston, accession 23.272.

37. The illustration "Death of Georg Wilhelm Richmann" is from the 1863 book *Les Grand Inventions,* by Louis F. Guier. It is in the public domain because its copyright has expired.

38. The 1933 Goudey baseball card of Tony Lazzeri is in the public domain because it was published in the United States between 1923 and 1963 and although there may or may not have been a copyright notice, the copyright was not renewed.

39. The 2016 photograph of Pigeon Point Lighthouse, Pescadero, California, is copyright © by Frank Schulenberg, and is used here under CC BY-SA 4.0. It has been cropped.

40. The painting of a Russian train is from the 1913 book *Provincial Russia,* by Stewart Hugh and F. De Haenen (London: A. and C. Black). It is in the public domain because its copyright has expired.

41. The 1936 photo of a soda jerk was taken by Alan Fisher, staff photographer for the *New York World-Telegram and Sun* (NYWTS). It is part of the NYWTS collection donated to the Library of Congress (digial ID cph.3c13825), and is in the public domain per the instrument of gift.

42. The 19th century advertisement for Hires Root Beer is in the public domain because its copyright has expired.

43. The painting *Christmas Pie* by William Henry Hunt was created prior to 1864, and is in the public domain because its copyright has expired.

44. The 1866 painting *Jar of Peaches* by Claude Monet is in the New Masters Gallery, Dresden, Germany, accession NM-2525-B-PS01. It is in the public domain because its copyright has expired.

45. The painting *Transfiguration of Jesus* by Raphael was created prior to 1521, and is in the public domain because its copyright has expired.

46. The 1943 photograph of a Buffalo, New York, nursery school for children of working mothers was taken by Marjory Collins for the Office of War Information. It is in the public domain as a work created by an employee of the US federal government as part of that person's official duties. The

original photo is in the collection of the Library of Congress, digital ID fsa.8d18633.

47. The Kenny's Roasted Coffee trading card of a girl and her doll was created circa 1900 by C. D. Kenny stores, and is from the Shields Trade Cards Collection at Miami University Libraries (accession no. 798). It is in the public domain because its copyright has expired.

48. The painting "August" is from the *Brevarium Grimani,* circa 1510, and is in the public domain because its copyright has expired.

49. The 1815 woodcut of a proposal is in the public domain because its copyright has expired.

50. The photograph of an emerald cut peridot was taken by Michelle Jo, who released it into the public domain in 2009.

51. The photograph of the Cup of the Ptolemies was taken by "Clio20" and is used here under CC BY-SA 3.0. The cup is in the collection of the Bibliothèque Nationale de France.

52. The 1886 paintings *Vase with Cornflowers and Poppies* by Vincent van Gogh are in the public domain because its copyright has expired.

53. The 1886 painting *Vase with Red Gladioli* by Vincent van Gogh is in the public domain because its copyright has expired.

54. The 1886 painting *Vase with Cornflowers and Poppies* by Vincent van Gogh is in the public domain because its copyright has expired.

55. The 1896 illustration *August* by Eugène Grasset is in the public domain because its copyright has expired.

56. The celestial sphere is from *Scenography of the Ptolemaic Cosmography,* by Johannes van Loon, based on Andreas Cellarius's *Harmonia Macrocosmica,* 1660. It is in the public domain because its copyright has expired.

57. The 1906 automobile calendar is by Edward Penfield, and is in the collection of the Library of Congress Prints and Photographs Division. It is in the public domain because its copyright has expired.

58. The 50-year perpetual calendar photograph is in the public
    domain.

59. The cartoon by John T. McCutcheon is from his 1905
    collection *The Mysterious Stranger and Other Cartoons* by John
    T. McCutcheon. It is in the public domain because its
    copyright has expired.

60. The painting *August* by Joachim von Sandrart is in the
    public domain because its copyright has expired. The
    original can be found in the Staatsgalerie im Neuen Schloss,
    Schleißheim, Germany.

61. The painting *August* by Hans Thoma is from his book
    Festkalender. It is in the public domain because its copyright
    has expired.

Timespinner
Press

License Description and Terms

Aside from material purely in the public domain, photographs and other material in this book are used under specific licenses permitting free use, usually with an attribution requirement. For full text and terms of these licenses, click or enter the appropriate links below. If you believe there is an error in the copyright status or attribution of any of these images, please email us.

- Creative Commons Attribution 2.0 Generic (CC-BY 2.0): http://creativecommons.org/licenses/by/2.0/deed.en
- Creative Commons Attribution-Share Alike 3.0 Generic (CC-BY-SA 3.0): http://creativecommons.org/licenses/by-sa/3.0/
- Creative Commons Attribution-Share Alike 2.5 Generic (CC-BY-SA 2.5): http://creativecommons.org/licenses/by-sa/2.5/deed.en
- Creative Commons Attribution-Share Alike 2.0 Generic (CC-BY-SA 2.0): http://creativecommons.org/licenses/by/2.0/deed.en
- Creative Commons Attribution-Share Alike 1.0 Generic (CC-BY-SA 1.0): http://creativecommons.org/licenses/by-sa/1.0/deed.en
- CC0 1.0 Universal (CC0 1.0) Public Domain Dedication (CC0 1.0) http://creativecommons.org/publicdomain/zero/1.0/deed.en
- GNU Free Documentation License (GFDL): http://en.wikipedia.org/wiki/Wikipedia:Text_of_the_GNU_Free_Documentation_License
- License Art Libre (Free Art License): http://artlibre.org

August, by Joachim von Sandrart

Other Books from Timespinner Press

Timespinner
Press

The Story of a Special Day

Michael Dobson

A series of (eventually) 366 volumes covering everything that happened on your special day! Events, births, deaths, quotes, holidays, and much more. It's like a birthday card they'll never throw away!

US$7.95 print / US$2.99 ebook.

From Plassey to Pakistan

Humayun Mirza

The history of British Colonial India and the formation of Pakistan from the unique perspective of the son of Pakistan's first president and last of the royal line of Bengal, Bihar, and Orissa! This unique historical document tells the inside story of this distinguished family, including the detailed story of the coup that toppled his father from power!

US$27.95 print

A Whole New Navy: America's War in the Pacific

Miles Durr

The most comprehensive and detailed description of America's naval war in the Pacific ever—every battle, every ship, every task force and every task group from Pearl Harbor through the Japanese surrender! A must-have for the collection of every World War II buff!

US$29.95 print

Improbable History: The Weird, the Obscure, and the Strangely Important

edited by Michael Dobson

From the birth of Western civilization to the rescue of Apollo 13, from the Leaning Tower of Pisa to Florence's Duomo, history has often turned on small, improbable details. Whatever happened to the ancient Samaritan people? Why did a fortuitous rainstorm allow the British to conquer India? How did an air raid in Italy lead to the development of chemotherapy? What happened when Albert Einstein met Adolf Hitler on the streets of Berlin? How did the Japanese manage to attack the US mainland using balloons? A cast of award-winning writers tackle some of the strangest tales in history!

US$19.95 print

The Letters of William Philip Schwartz 1842-1855

edited by John F. Schwartz

The 19th century soldier and adventurer William Philip Schwartz wrote a series of vivid and detailed letters chronicling his adventures in the Indian Wars, the Mexican-American War, the Gold Rush, and his term as Marine sergeant aboard the USS Constellation. A pioneer in photography, he took *the first known war photographs*. An unforgettable first-hand look into life in the 19th century!

US$17.95 print

Watergate Considered as an Organization Chart of Semi-Precious Stones (and other essays)

by Michael Dobson

In this light-hearted yet insightful tour through the Nixon White House, the Committee to Re-Elect the President, and the various investigative committees, you'll meet fascinating characters from Richard Nixon himself to such lieutenants as a G. Gordon Liddy and John Dean. You'll gain insights into the origin of the scandal, the motives of the players, and how the situation spiraled so badly out of control.

US$9.95 print/US$3.99 ebook

August, by Hans Thoma